I0006421

Women's Guide to Men...
Updated Dating Advice &
Tips for Online Daters!

By International Bestselling Author on
Suicide & Behavioral Therapist:
Dr. Jacob K. Ray, M.A., Psy.D.

Introduction to Men-

Are you ready to finally get your man? Let me guide you straight to the best possible guy for you. I promise you success and happiness IF you listen closely and follow the steps. We are going to cover every single factor that needs to go into your decision. You will need to examine yourself in this process. I don't know you. Therefore, I am in no position to judge or condemn you for your past poor selections of guys. I can assume that your purchase of this future bestseller is some indication that you are open to a real relationship and are of age to decide something as important as your future and safety. You might have had experience(s) that make you feel like you need to research contemporary males. This book will leave no stone unturned. There will also be an emphasis on online dating. This book is a cry for a return to the days of real families that lasted and stayed together. Divorce plagues our society. The tears from the children of divorce could drown the world. That is enough of a reason for me to write this to help you avoid meeting that future divorcer, beater, deserter, or cheater. I will start with guys to avoid using what I call the Red Flag System. Once we safely push them to the side, we will discuss how to read men's behavior. Then, we will put you under the microscope. We will conclude with fail-proof tips on how to dress for and conduct yourself on dates. The great news is we have you on board. Love conquers all, unfortunately.

It conquers logic, reason, and safety sometimes. That is why and how you ladies end up in severely bad relationships with loser guys. You are far too forgiving and kind. I will teach you to loathe that guy you tolerate who treats you like garbage. I will unveil his true colors and make you go blind from the light of truth. But, if I show you and you stay with him, that is on you. If every single person in your life is telling you to end your relationship or dump your current lousy guy but you won't do it, pass this book to a friend. I can't help you. If you are not willing to come to the other island, not the one you live on, but the new one, then don't cross the waters. Stay put and stay unhappy. If you are ready to dive in and get the right guy for you instead of saying to yourself, "He's not the one but he'll do for now." Then, turn the page. If you are tired of explaining your current love interest's outbursts to friends and family or making excuses for his inane behavior, keep reading. If you are unhappy and in the same dead end relationship but impossible to reach out to when it comes to your own rights to be happy, read no further. Like everybody else who has tried, I can't do anything with you either. Women who are in boring, unfulfilling, or once nostalgic relationships that have soured with a high school sweetheart who has bored you to death and robbed you of your youth but you stay anyway, this book won't work for you. Nothing will. Anyone blinded by love cannot be given new eyes. They have to be willing to open the ones they have, even if it means cringing at what they see they've settled for.

Chapter 1- The Red Flag System

So, you like men? Great! Let's make sure you pick the safest, healthiest, most emotionally available one. The fastest way to do this is to use Red Flags. What does a Red Flag mean? When you go to the beach and the waves are deadly they fly the Red Flag as a warning for hazardous or unsafe conditions. The Red Flag lets beachgoers know to stay away. If somebody jumps in the ocean and drowns people say, "They should have known to stay out. There was a Red Flag." Exact same thing with guys. You might jump in and make it out. But, you are a lot more likely to drown. A Red Flag symbolizes danger or a poor investment. We will use the Red Flag system to warn you of danger or your time being poorly utilized. If you are the kind of girl who looks at the exterior of a house and makes an offer without going inside to check it out thoroughly then you are lost and red flags abound. Don't let good looking, rich, smooth talking guys fool you with shallow gifts or attributes. Looks fade. Personality does not. Go deeper and you will be swimming in options. I am going to reel you in now to the work part of the book. Grab a notepad and take your own notes. Heck, keep a journal if you like. Write a blog about it and make a movie with me in it! Just be sure to get involved with writing or recording your thoughts about what kind of guy and relationship you want. Do you want kids? Do you already have kids? Do you want marriage? Do you want a long term boyfriend, husband, or boy toy? What do you want? Decide now before reading the whole book. But, let's start with the easy guys to eliminate from your list:

#1 RED FLAG! The Hardcore Addict-Ladies? The guys who drink or drug heavy and never cut back are lost causes. The hardcore addict is not a suitable mate. In nature, he would not survive. Think about picking a survivor. The addict that can't or won't quit or cut back is never worth your time. They will use pity, seduction, manipulation, suicidal threats, and sometimes homicidal threats to lure you in to the enabler position. Don't wait around for some dude to miraculously change who does speed all day and lives paycheck to paycheck. Hardcore drinkers come in many forms. Alcoholism does not discriminate. Any guy of any social grouping can be an alcoholic. Some will never drink heavily around you. Others will hide their drinking completely. Some are much more out in the open but they just drink wine. Wine drinkers are as much of a drunk as any other drunk out there. Don't let the wine expert guy you met on Match dot com fool you. If he is pounding glass after glass of anything, no matter how old or rare, he is an alcoholic. Not sure if the dater you're with is a drunk? Watch them. Do they tend to have two drinks at a time or do they order another beer before finishing every drop of their current beer? Do they drink liquor and pound shots? Still not sure? Count the number and type of drinks they have over the course of a night. Any guy who drinks into the double digits, that is, more than nine drinks is trouble. Stay away. Money, class, potency, and looks are never a worthy exchange for your dream guy or the mate you want to sire your offspring and worship at your feet. This is your man, your beautiful man. Don't let a sad addict take his place. Give the one you currently are with one shot to clean up his act, for good. If he fails after six months or has one relapse, move forward. If you are an addict, you cannot continue this book until you get help. The book will be here, don't worry. Go take care of YOURSELF first. Don't drag anybody else into the mess you've made. Women who are addicts are just as pitiful as the men. Break the cycle. Revisit love after you've learned to love yourself. If you don't love yourself you will mirror that in your relationships. Look around. Evidence is everywhere. Women who seek out addicts are contending poorly with their own issues of worth. Leave the addict guys alone. They are an unreachable fruit from a diseased tree. Bite into their bittersweet center and see for yourself. If you make a puckered face and go back for another gnaw at his poison, he will have time to lure you to his web and suck out your passion. Don't bother with the heavy drinker, the druggy, the wine expert, master beer brewer, bar owner, the pill poppers, injection junkies, and powder sniffers. They are more trouble than they are worth. They unilaterally make for a lousy parent, lousy lover, they are chronically depressed and if that still isn't enough, picture them dying in the hospital from overindulgence. That should do it.

2 Red Flag- The Arrogant Good-Looking Jerk: I know you think he is gorgeous. He has money. He has the nicest things and shares them with you. He carries you through life by footing the bill and you tolerate him. Oh sure, he can be nice, especially in the beginning. But, be forewarned: he is only doing enough to lure you in. Once he has you for long enough that jerk persona will take over. If you are smiling to yourself because you are in that spot right now, get rid of him. Looks fade. Personality does not. If you have issues of worth around your looks and think your man is a prize catch even though you hate the way he is about everything, you need to drop him. Get out. The Arrogant Good looking Jerk will belittle you. He will talk down to you and remind you of your place. He will make you think you are lucky to be with him but you will eventually come to hate the prison he keeps you in. He is the guy that calls his wife fat while she is still losing weight after a pregnancy. This guy will never

change. He will replace you and blame you for the relationship ending and you will walk away wondering if some things he said were true? Good news! They are not. He is a jerk. You figured him out after wasting time hoping the nice guy he was in the beginning would reappear. He does that to every woman. He will never stop or change. Move forward.

3 Red Flag- The Relationship Addict- This is the guy from a string of marriages, divorces, relationships, or chronic first dates. He is indecisive. Leave him alone. Anybody who goes from relationship to relationship without a break has no to low self-esteem. They are like an addict. The drug is feeling needed or loved. These guys may have a lot going for them but if they talk about the countless failed relationships they have been in, guess what? They are in those relationships for the wrong reasons with the wrong women. Don't let your name get added to his list. If the guy has been married more than twice and/or has no lapse between relationships fly the Red Flag and politely excuse yourself from him. Other tell-tale signs of the relationship addict include: secrecy and vagueness around

past relationships, secrecy and vagueness around how intimate said past relationships were, secrecy and vagueness around why they are interested in <u>you</u> and/or inadequate explanations for why past relationships failed. Pay careful attention to how he reacts when you ask him how long he stayed single before dating you. If there was no lapse at all, red flag. Everybody needs time to lick their wounds and mourn the loss of a relationship gone sour. If the guy sitting across from you that you met on eharmony tells you he just got divorced a month ago, bail. He might be an addict. If he goes on and on about how important it is that he has someone to spend time with, all the time, know that he can't tolerate being alone. These guys wear you out with neediness and leave your dried husk to blow away in the breeze. They got what they needed from you: a fix. Don't get duped. If the guy you have been dating for less than two years starts asking you to move in and marry, be careful. He might be addicted to relationships, not you. You might be the sucker he has been waiting for since the one before you figured him out and left. Pay close attention to what he attributes his past relationship's endings to. If he says things like, "I guess we just weren't meant to be" or "we just grew apart" be careful. Those are vague, ambiguous responses. A more concrete and genuine response would be "I wanted children. She did not." The relationship addict can come in many forms. He may be a great catch on the surface. But, don't let your lust blind you to his past. If it sounds like the ones before you left him and not the other way around, be careful. If he professes his love for you too early or goes above and beyond in the romance department, particularly with trying to buy your affection, be warned. That stuff is endearing then creepy. If you do not reciprocate his over-the-top gestures of romance, he might leave you. But, chances are he will guilt-trip you successfully like he did the ones before you and then you're stuck with him. Don't become the fix or the fixer-upper. You can't mold this guy. No one else has been able to. If you want to give it a shot, the book will be waiting for you when he's finished with you or you with him. The relationship addict can be female, too. If you have never been single, you are one. If you literally go from relationship to relationship, without stopping in between to do self-care and repair, you are no different than him. Women who cannot be single have issues of worth they are contending with poorly. You all know her. She's the girl who goes from dumping or getting dumped right back to the bars and clubs to fill the void. She cannot live one breath without some dude drooling over her. These women need to get to a behavioral therapist immediately. If you are guilty of being in relationships to be needed or loved by just any guy that will take the job, you might be an addict. Relationship addicts have no identity outside of the couple. They are the ones who only talk about themselves in relation to their partner. That's why they get on our nerves. You only hear about their relationship and the things they did as a pair. The addict has no individual identity. He or she cannot exist alone. They do not have adequate self-esteem to do so. So, they attach themselves to the hip of their partner. If the guy you are into has no life outside of you, get out. Find someone with boundaries and separation. If you are reading this and thinking "Yeah, but I want a guy to spend every waking moment with. I want my guy to be crazy about me. I want my guy to give me as much attention as he can." That is fine. But, you will probably get smothered over time. Give this book to a friend if he gets you. Healthy relationships need boundaries and some separation. I will talk more about that later but for now just know that I feel you but I'm telling you too much togetherness is cancer on healthy bonding. You will smother each other and learn to call that happiness. Don't. There is so much more to real, authentic, genuine love. If you want to play house with some guy, any guy, who comes along who fits the bill, then, I can't help you. You can be picky. You have the right to choose from the billions of males who are alive right now and single. Don't pick the one guy who smothers, uses you up, and spits you out. He won't shed a tear over you when you end it. He will simply replace you and move on.

#4 Red Flag- Mr. Fuddy-Duddy a.k.a. The Guy-who-is-too-steady. This is the guy who has everything: he is stable with career and money, he looks good enough for you, he has friends and hobbies that create healthy separation in your relationship, he is romantic enough, he takes you out once a week to dinner, he even brings flowers sometimes. So, what's the problem? He is BORING. You have heard all of his stories, met all his friends, gone out to all those dinners and you might even love him. But, ladies? If you are bored with him now what makes you think that will ever change? Personality is fixed. Boring, too steady-too perfect or stereotypically romantic guys are okay but why settle? If you are constantly thinking to yourself how boring your life is, do something. Boredom is another cancer on relationships. By the time you get away from him, your girlfriends will make fun of you for staying with Mr. Fuddy-Duddy for so long. If your guy is a drag, your life is a drag. Don't stay foolishly hoping he will all of a sudden morph into Mr. Excitement. Stability is great and is a cornerstone of health in relationships. That does not mean you have to be bored or stay bored. If you guys stay home on Friday nights and he gets up from the couch at eleven and says, "I'm beat. I'm going to bed" and a wave of disgust washes over you as you stay up to watch tv and drink another bottle of wine as he snores loudly in the next room then you are bored. If you think to yourself how jealous you are of all your girlfriends who have lively, funny, interesting, and fun loving guys they are with and you don't, you are stuck with Mr. Dud, then, get out. Test the waters. Next Friday night instead of waiting for him to go to bed at eleven sharp, get up. Call your girls and go out with them. If you have more fun than you've had the entire time you have been with Mr. Boring, then get out of that relationship. Get one of your girlfriends to fix you up with one of her boy's friends who goes out with them all the time. If you feel like your relationship is causing you to miss out on life, it is. End it. Now.

5 Red Flag- The Stalker or Annoying guy-who-won't-let-you-go & other assorted crazies. Sometimes he is hard to spot. He can even decide to not stalk you if you end it right. He is scary, annoying, and unbelievably pathetic but most of all <u>dangerous</u>. Stalking is an act of terrorism. He should be treated as

such. Any guy you meet who is an enigma when it comes to their past is a bad pick. Stalkers are usually men with Borderline Personality Disorder traits. What does that mean? It means they have no separation between themselves and you, once they attach to you. To him, you are either a savior or an abandoner. Your position changes at any given time depending on his emotional valence. If you start seeing a guy and he is over-the-top jealous, has serious road rage, is possessive, suspicious of your fidelity or violent to anyone, get out. You should screen any guys you date anyway, especially if you are bold enough to date online. Nothing frightens me more than to think you would use a big name, reputable online dating service and think they check out every guy who signs up. There's no way. Stalkers are psychotic. They live in a fantasy world. The Internet is like a dream come true for them. They can sign up, just like you did for that dating website. I think it should be required that each applicant submit to a background check. But, even a background check is no guarantee. Stalkers have restraining orders taken out on them and they still stalk. What on earth makes you think having that background check is enough? You have to watch out for the warning signs, too. Ask questions. Record responses. Judge responses carefully. Be sure to include questions about: any and all history of mental health services they have received or have been court ordered to receive, any and all history of violence, any and all history of arrests, any and all history of incarceration, any and all history of domestic violence and/or substance abuse. Guys who are pushy about sex or who have degrading sex fetishes or sex practices (including rough dirty talk and all violent acts during sex) that dominate your sex life are bad stock. If you are getting to know some guy who just got out of jail and he turns around and stalks you after you figure out he's nuts then you need help, too. Women who go for stalkers are not without flaw, unless you are a celebrity and are being stalked that way. Women who like bad boys or the mysterious quiet types are most likely to get stalked. Stalkers may not be violent. They might just be annoying. There are varying degrees of stalking. The guy you dumped who shows up a week later at your apartment, drunk, in the middle of the night, with his buddies waiting in the car as he begs you back one last time is the low end of the scale. The guy who comes by once a month after you broke up to "hang out" because you said you could "still be friends" is the next step. He will eventually twist and distort things to make himself think you want him back. The guy who calls and texts and emails over and over is the third step up the stalker ladder. He just won't get it. It is over. You said so. He can't let it go. He begs and bugs. If he thinks you've moved on or are dating someone new he gets ugly and reminds you why you ended it with him. The constant caller/emailer/texter is pretty creepy. Change your phone number, ladies. Tell people you lost your phone. It happens all the time. If he keeps emailing you, block him or filter his emails to the trash. If he writes you from another email address, close that email. Never give any guy your work email. Never. Why? Because if you give a guy that email and he turns out to be crazy, you can't just close that email account to stop his emails. Always get a free yahoo email account that does not have your first and last name in it. That way, you have an email just for your lovelife. Set your Facebook profile to private or use your middle name or a nickname. Persistent guys you reject will invent reasons to contact you online. Don't bite, if they hit you up. It sends a mixed message to their little deluded male brain. They will see it as a green light. Keep flying the red flag instead. Don't mix business with pleasure. If you gave a coworker or some guy in your field your business card and he is using that as a way to hit on you, put a stop to it. If you are interested in him, give him your free yahoo email. Don't let guys blur boundaries in the beginning. They will build on it. Stalkers will feed off of it. Other crazies to avoid include: any guy with any history of violence or who has tons of piercings and tattoos is a bad choice. Tattoos and piercings are neat. But, the real truth is that guy who has tons of them is crazy. They are mutilating their bodies after a certain point. Fact. I don't care what the excuse is tons of piercings and tats equals mutilator with insecurities. The type of insecurities that lead to problems. I'm just saying, guys who have tons of them have to be crazy to do that. If you disagree, your crazy.

Any guys who threaten people are bad news. Guys who used to or still get into fights, arguments, or who are heavy into martial arts, UFC (Ultimate Fighting), or weapons of any kind are crazy. Guys who play videogames where killing, stealing, and raping are considered fun are insane especially the Grand Theft Auto gamers and first person shooter gamers. Hello girls? Those guys are practicing how to be sociopaths using their gaming consoles and computers! Do you really need a psychological research panel to confirm that they are nuts? Guys who say really creepy, weird, or unnerving things when you express interest in ending the relationship are to be avoided. Ladies, if I were you, I would screen every guy I dated as thoroughly as possible especially if you met online. I recommend based solely on this section, that you try to get fixed up with guys that are trustworthy and have been known by your friends for years. In other words, if you are single and you think your girlfriend's neighbor in her apartment complex is cute and you know she has known him for years, see if she can fix you up with him instead of going online and rolling the dice. The dating sites might promise safety and careful screening but stalkers know how to cheat the system. Any guy who says even jokingly that they will stalk you if you break it off with them is not worth staying with. Ladies, I love you, each and all, but you are going to have to be hypervigilant with guys in the beginning. I'm not saying to go out and have a bad time because you can't relax wondering if this guy from Chemistry dot com is a serial killer or not but what I am saying is don't tell him too much about: where you hang out, exactly, who you know by first and last name, where you work, exactly, your physical address or neighborhood, your private cell phone number (get his number and block yours when you call, until he proves he is safe, that way if things don't work out, he can email you but at least he can't call you) or anything else too revealing. If he is a stalker his brain is recording those facts for use later. How did he know where you worked? You probably told him on the first or second date and forgot. How did he find you at your favorite margarita bar that you and your girlfriends go to every Tuesday for the special on frozen pitchers? You probably told him early on. Don't tell guys details like that. Just say, I work downtown or I work in advertising NOT I work on Lombard Street and Third in that old grey building with the stone eagle on top at Wordsmith & Longfellow Advertising Firm. Details are like footholds in the climb up Crazy Mountain with stalkers. Be careful with guys who make you feel uneasy in the beginning. If that new guy you are dating seems too hidden or too perfect think: potential weirdo stalker. Guys who check up on you or who are pushy about exact details and exact information about what you do, where you are all day everyday, where you live and who you spend time with are too nosey. That stuff is none of their business, unless you let them pressure you into telling them. You have every right in the first six to eight months to withhold any detailed information about yourself if you met your guy online. If you got set up through a friend and they know and love this guy and think you are a good match then you can be more forthcoming. Otherwise, err on the side of caution. I could not live with myself if one of you got hurt. I love you all. You are the mothers of our kind. And, I hate that there are crazy and dangerous guys out there but there are. Remember: the way he handles anger, sexual rejection, rejection, and jealousy are all cues as to whether or not you have a potential stalker or other assorted crazy on your hands. Pay close attention to his sexual behavior also. If he has a foot fetish or likes for you to whip him or he is into rough or degrading sex, he is crazy. Daily porn watchers are a bad choice. Listen to your gut. If sex is a compromise for you, meaning you kinda just go along with his strange requests and fetishes to get him off, get out. That's not right. Its creepy. If your guy is on any psychiatric medication, any dose, any drug, stay away. If he has any history of violence or is into weapons, takes or teaches martial arts, stay away. If he plays video games where the fun part is murdering, stealing, raping, and blowing things up, he is a sociopath in training. Stay away. If he threatens people a lot or is a total road raging lunatic when you are in the car, stay away. If he says he used to get into fights or still does or has any involvement with the legal system around violence, domestic violence, or anger management, stay away. If he has women coming over to his house with family members to confront him or he moves a lot, stay away. If he has <u>no friends</u> or is isolative in a creepy, paranoid way, stay away. If he goes on and on about being in therapy his whole life or comes from a severely abusive home, stay away. If he has ever gone to jail over anything for any amount of time, stay away. We don't date jailbirds. If he makes you feel scared for your safety when he gets angry during arguments, end the relationship. Use your gut. If he is weird on the first date and creepy on the second, don't sleep with him, dummy! If he won't stop calling, emailing, facebooking, myspacing, texting, tweeting, or showing up at your house, job, or hang out then call the cops. Get a restraining order. Move and change jobs. Your life is worth it. If he follows you everywhere you go, buy a gun. If he still won't take a hint, call me and I'll kick his ass! I want you to be safe, happy, respected, cared for, held, loved, and cherished. I won't allow you to be unhappy, unfulfilled, bored, or abused. Stalkers should be locked up and the key should be thrown away. They are unreachable, scary, psychotic, and annoying. Pay attention to their life story in the beginning. If it is riddled with violence, abuse, substance abuse, bad relationships, bad parents, trauma, legal problems of any kind, or seems too polished to be true, stay away. Severe problems and struggles are a recipe for craziness. These guys may look good on the surface but if he has a smile on his face as he tells you all about how his Dad used to beat the shit out of him when he was a kid but that it just made him stronger, stay away. I would say to use common sense but as I said earlier most of you ladies are too kind and forgiving. Don't let your pity blind you to the reality that guys who come from really hardcore backgrounds are fucked up from it. Let someone else take them on. Don't try to fix him or give him support. Let society have him. He will end up where he belongs: in jail, court ordered anger management, or rehab/ therapy. Guys who were victims of child abuse are different but they carry scars.

Trust your gut with them. Know that they can harbor rage. If you love him and feel for him, get him the help he needs to learn to channel that anger. Leave the scrappers and bruisers, video gaming killers, druggies, broke-hipster drunk punk rockers, gang idiots, thugs, and UFC-wannabe nutjobs alone. They are all crazy. I'm telling you right here, right now. Any dude with any violent or addiction anything ain't worth it. Any guy who punches or throws things when they get mad or who screams at the top of their lungs during arguments is a powder keg. Don't carry lit matches around their fuse, stay away from them in the first place.

Chapter Summary:

The Red Flag system has been introduced by using my examples from clinical lore. Now, you need to take out that notepad and write down at least five or ten of your own Red Flags. You may hate the smell of cigarettes, a Red Flag for you would be Smokers. You might not want the guy who drinks Apple Martinis or girlie drinks, you may want the traditional beer chugging guy, that could be a Red Flag. You might be into guys who are in great shape, that might be a Red Flag if the guy from online is frumpy. Whatever it is you dislike or are turned off about, list it now. Use your Red Flags in shaping your decisions. No guy is perfect but that does not mean you should look the other way if they are crazy or unhealthy. Remember: we want a <u>survivor</u>. We want a guy who would be able to survive in nature. Society shields us from so many dangers in the world, but ladies, that does not mean the world can't snowball on you and your relationship. Don't pick someone of weak character with chaos and disorder all over their lives and expect my techniques to work. Recruit a real man who has battled but lived to tell about it. I want you to get that guy who is kind, rugged, strong, tough, loving, tender, thoughtful, patient, sensitive and at ease. If you pick the good looking angry jerk, addict guy, heavy body altering guy, boring guy, relationship hopper, player guy, broke artist-rocker guy, fetish guy or the stalker and stay with him, then don't complain to those of us who tried to warn you or stear you to safer shores. Happiness is a right and a practice. If

you surround yourself with well
adjusted, kind, loving, but acceptably
imperfect fellas who are at ease with
life, you will be fulfilled. Ignore the Red
Flags, leave things to chance or get
blinded by lust or greed for his money or
things and you are just as lost as he is
and you deserve each other. Break
away from the misers of the world and
the violent guys and the jealous guys
and the angry guys and your man will
emerge like a Phoenix from the ashes.
Stay with your current relationship out of
habit or stay single because you are
afraid and you will miss that beautiful
bird as he takes you under his wing and
whisks you away to his castle in the sky.
Don't let family and friends tell you to
stay for the kids if you have children but
are unhappy with your marriage. You
are doing them a disservice. That was a
tip given to me by my old mentor during
my training. He had been a therapist for
over forty years. Listen to me: your
staying in the marriage for the kids is a
disservice to them. End your current
shitty relationship now so you can have
a chance at a better life. The book will
be here waiting for you whenever you
are ready. But, know that once you buy

in to my system, there is no going back. Swim to my island and know that you can stay, if you follow the rules. The first goal is to get you making safe time investments when getting to know potential keepers. That is, I just taught you who to avoid and why, now you must find a potential keeper and get to know him. The rest will fall into place. If you still are uncertain, take a moment to picture your own funeral. Go ahead. See yourself in that coffin, dead. Now, float around listening to what people are saying. Do they think that you stayed with that jerk of a husband out of love? For the kids? Or because you truly loved him? Listen carefully to what they are saying about you as you lay there, dead. Do you like what you are hearing? Is it true? False? Why did you stay, when everybody else could see how miserable you were? If you are reaching for a tissue, I've made my point. If you are okay with what they said about you, then you can give the book to a friend now. My gut tells me you are either single or there was a question mark floating over your relationship and you hoped reading this would help answer it. It will. But, you have to be honest with yourself. I can give you a skeleton. Its up to you to flesh it out.

Chapter 2- Men's Behavior and how to interpret it

1. In the beginning...Ladies? Your guy
   in the beginning is when he is on his
   best behavior. If he is a handful right
   off the bat, drop him. You are getting
   him at his best when you first meet.
   If he is a pain in the ass but you are
   still intrigued because you want to
   make sure and it is sort of flattering
   that he keeps calling or emailing you,
   know that a pain now is a bigger pain
   later. Drop him. Guys who come off
   perfect in the beginning and sweep
   you off your feet are almost always
   hiding or overcompensating for
   something. Guys who bombard you
   with demands to spend more and
   more time together after you just met
   are not worth it. They are probably a
   relationship addict and you missed it
   the first three dates. If he calls you
   and you see that its him and you let
   it go to voicemail, drop him. That little
   voice that says "I don't want to talk to
   him right now" will just get louder and
   more frequent the longer you let him
   get you on the phone every time he
   calls. If you feel annoyed when you

politely text him back and he texts you back immediately with a message that requires a response from you, know that if he is doing that in the beginning, it will only get worse. The "constant contact" guy is never going to get better. They are insecure within themselves and need your constant validation. Don't give it to them. End the relationship. The guy who leaves stuff at your house (like a video you wanted to see) and uses that as a reason to call or come over to keep constant contact with you is a prime example. Don't borrow anything from guys. Don't leave anything you own at their house. They will use it as an excuse to call you after you break it off. Guys will invent any excuse they can to call you after you end it, literally. If you have anything at their place, know that to a guy, its like gold because now they have the perfect excuse to call you. The beginning is the best and the worst part of the relationship. The best part is being blinded by love. The worst part is kicking yourself later on when things went south because you knew he was that way but you didn't care or try to stop yourself. It happens all the time. The first year and a half is bliss. Then, you start seeing the real person. If you can refrain from getting blinded too early then I can help you avoid that day months or years later where you are kicking yourself for staying with him for so long when you knew all along he was not the right guy for you. Men in the beginning know to behave. If they do not or cannot act right, consider that an early sign from the universe telling you to move on.

2. I'm not sure how he feels about me...aka The Player. Okay, let's take the Player's game playing behaviors and let me interpret. For instance, a guy you met recently and had sex with calls to hang out and you get ready to go. He calls back and reschedules. Guess what? You aren't the only girl he is sleeping with. You are in a rotation with no telling how many other girls. A better option for the night popped up in the interim and you lost out to the other girl. Guys who are just having sex with you and "hanging out" are players, ladies. Trust me. If you don't think so

ask him details about what he did the night he cancelled on you. Watch him squirm in his seat and stammer. Other sure signs of a player include: any guy who is secretive about texting or typing while using any cell phone, computer or internet enabled device or who steps out to make or take phone calls and you just started hooking up with them. Any guy who lies to you or gives you the vibe that they are lying is a liar. Like Chris Rock, my favorite comedian, says, "Men are only as faithful as their options." If you have been added to a player's list of girls know that you are somewhere on that totem pole but the totem pole never comes down. Players will add and replace girls on their rotations and you never know where you stand. Some girls are devastated when they catch their new so-called "boyfriend" texting some chick. I say you should have seen it coming. Players don't apologize. They use the "But, I told you I was single!" excuse to screw as many girls as they can. Players won't take you to certain places, even though they talk about them.

For example, they might mention the sports bar where they drink with their boys. You might think nothing of it when actually he and his guy friends try to take girls home from that bar every Friday and laugh about it to each other behind your back. Show up there one night unannounced and see what he does. If you haven't caught him chatting up some girl, he will get furious. But, if he is genuine, he will be happy you stopped by. If you are okay with both of you being with other partners as you get to know each other, that's fine. But, if months and months go by and he doesn't try to get closer to you, he is playing you. Players are uncertain about commitment but they are certain about wanting to get laid by as many different girls as possible. Players will break your heart. Some will even tell you they love you just to keep having sex with you. Others will dump you as soon as you ask for anything from them. It might hurt but you need to let him go. These guys are the ones later on who cheat on you after y'all have been married for ten years and they get bored. You can't take a lion out of the jungle and make him into a house cat. Players have already figured out there are enough gullible, vulnerable, and willing sex partners for them to prey upon. You were just part of a rotation. Any guy who won't call you unless you call them or who avoids you after just spending a weekend having sex with you is screwing someone else this weekend. Your turn will come around again next weekend, maybe. Players always update their roster. If you are too needy or too much trouble or won't stop calling, texting, emailing, and facebooking them you will get dropped. Don't let it hurt. Just move on. Players also carefully remove any evidence of any other girl being at their house before you come over. The spider must make his web. Guys know to hide the other girl's toothbrush or thong panties before you get there. If he keeps a stash of condoms right near the bed, next time he leaves to go to the bathroom, count them. Next time you go over, wait until he goes to the bathroom and count them again.

Keep doing that if you're suspicious. You will catch him eventually. If you go out somewhere and he wants to leave all of a sudden it is because the place you are in is too likely a place to run into one of the other girls he is sleeping with. If his eyes wander everywhere you go, no matter what you are wearing, you might have a player on your hands. The main thing to watch out for is his cell phone. If he is funny about it or gets super protective of it or turns the screen away from you, he is texting another girl. Guys will disguise girl's names in their phones, too. That way, if you do take it, there are no girl names in it. Its all guy names. Players lock their phones, too. If your new boyfriend ditches you frequently and blames work or friends he is probably screwing somebody else. If he lies about his whereabouts and you bust him lying, end the relationship. Any guy who is secretive or vague about what they did or who they were with or where they were is lying to you. You are being played or they are trying to drop a hint that you ain't the one for

them. Guys that you have to pursue
aren't worth the chase. Like Biggie
Smalls said, "Don't chase 'em,
replace 'em." Remember: no cologne
smells worse than desperation. If
you act desperate and needy its a
turn off no matter where you are in a
relationship. If you find yourself
constantly wondering when and if he
got your text or email or voicemail
that's a bad sign. Chances are you
are dependent on men for approval
and affection. You have to love
yourself first. A healthy balance of
him calling you and you calling him is
the goal. Too much of him calling and
too much of you calling is a bad sign.
Don't get played trying to just get
laid. And, don't try to take Lions out
of the jungle. Men communicate by
sex. If we are into you, we show it
with sex. If we avoid you or sex with
you, we are either bored or have
other sex partners who are better. If
you blow up guy's phones and
Facebook them constantly while
staying single and managing only to
hook up with players, you need to
stop and check yourself. There is
something missing about you. They

call it self-love. Learn to love yourself
first and the players will leave you
alone. They can sniff your
confidence and know you can't be
duped. Don't play their games, at all.
Get confident and let the good men
find you. Players are a stepping
stone for younger girls, get them out
of your system. They all look good,
smell good, act right, etc. But, they
are playing you. I'm sorry.

3. The "long term part" of long term
   relationships: these behaviors vary
   but some of the classics include not
   being as affectionate, not doing
   things around the house, arguing
   more intensely, not listening to you or
   acknowledging your feelings, not
   caring about your daily life, and not
   being romantic anymore. Men
   cannot fake it when the wind has
   been sucked out of their sails. If your
   guy has become impatient and
   demanding when he used to wait all
   day and ask nicely, then, your
   relationship has changed. If you
   guys were once a team around
   household chores but now you just
   do it all while he sits there watching
   football, then, things have changed.

If you used to brag about how loving and tender he was to your jealous girlfriends but now he is aloof and emotionally unavailable, then, things have changed. If every time you start to talk and he groans, sighs, or rolls his eyes when he used to perk up and be attentive, then, things have changed. If he doesn't even bother with flowers or decent gifts for you for your birthday when he used to give you really nice things, then, things have changed. Notice the pattern? If your guy is no longer who or how he was <u>things</u> <u>have</u> <u>changed</u>. List all of the ways he used to be and the way he is now. Confront him on it. Tell him you want change or you're done. If he blows you off or tells you to chill out, dump him. Guys will only work as much as they have to to get by in relationships. Tell him he better step it up or you're gone. If he doesn't fall to his knees begging you for another chance, leave him on that couch. People settle in relationships. We call it sacrifice. We call it compromise. I call it allowing unhealthy and unfulfilling patterns to form and solidify and then wondering what went wrong? The answer is always the same. You let things slide and build up and so did he. Now, you have a comfortable but convoluted mess you call love. Give him six months to turn it around or leave. You can't fix tedium. You can't tame a restless heart. If your man says he's unhappy with the way things are but when it comes right down to it he won't or can't change then shed your tears and say goodbye. Find a guy who is willing to change anytime it benefits the healthiness of the relationship. Get a partner not a player or a neutered bull. Guys who expect you to do it all are lazy. They are very likely to be depressed underneath all their logic. If you are frowning right now because that guy is sitting across the room in his recliner then give him one last shot to change or get out. This is your one and only life. This is not a video game. You don't get to do it over once you die. If your one and only life is miserable, even if it used to be happy, and it is largely due to changes in your relationship then change it. You make the choice everyday to put up with him. Choose not to, if he can't show some willingness and effort to get off his ass to salvage your love. If you need help go to a marriage counselor with a doctorate. Just know that usually if you are on a sinking ship trying to plug the leak or get all the water out, one bucketful at a time, and he isn't helping, that ship will sink. Counseling can at least tell you how big the hole is and if its worth plugging.

4. The Cheater/Deserter- these guys are self-explanatory. Easy to pick out. If your guy ever cheats on you, once, dump him or he will do it again. If you think he is fooling around but you're not sure just ask. Men's reactions to being accused of cheating will tell all. Extreme anger, stories that don't add up, and refusal to face facts about why you're suspicious are all signs of a cheater. Another easy way to catch them is to watch the show "Cheaters" together. Watch and listen to his reactions and responses to the cases they profile on the show. Guys who are cheating on you will squirm the whole time

that show is on. Ask them questions about the cases. If they offer pointers on how the guy could have avoided being caught, its because they know from personal experience! Any guy who admits to cheating in the past on any girl is a cheater. Any guy who has a girl that they spend more time with than you is probably cheating on you or wants to. Guys who hang out with ex girlfriends are cheaters or wannabe cheaters. Guys who have kids with another girl and use that as a reason to spend a lot of time away from you might have hopped over the fence on you. You never know until the shift happens. It can come out of nowhere. One day the cheater will snap. Something will give and they will lose it on you. That is the guilt eating away at them. Usually, it happens after they feel obligated to be with you but they really want their girl on the side. Eventually a decision will be made. I suggest you beat him to the punch. Guys who cheat have stories that don't add up. The excuses and amount of time they spend away from you and the way they explain that to you is critical in being able to sniff out a bonafide cheater. Another good way to tell if he is a cheater is to throw yourself at him sexually as soon as he walks in the door from being with the other girl. Most cheaters will fumble and babble and push you away. Its because they just orgasmed and aren't in the mood. If you do happen to get him nude take a whiff near his crotch. Does he smell like sex? Lube? That condom smell? He might have gone as far as to wash himself off down there but if he wreaks of sex or other unusually strong, uncharacteristic smells, he might have been cheating. Cheaters can be careless and stupid. Other cheaters can be impossible to bust. Either way, I have rarely encountered a female who suspected a male of cheating who has been wrong. The lying, time spent away from you, using the cell phone to assist in cheating by blaming signal strength or texting instead of calling, or any other feature on a computer or handheld device that enables them to lie easier and stay away from home base should be obvious enough. Sadly, there are countless women out there who live with dirty dogs. There are guys who you would never guess who cheat constantly and discreetly. Cheater guys can run the gamut from dumb to brilliant, lovable to loath-able, forgiveness worthy to death penalty candidates for what they have destroyed with their lies. Don't give him a second chance. Shed your tears and say goodbye. Cheaters who get away with it will never learn. Don't let him back into your life, not even for sex. The cheater is never worth trusting again. I don't care how nice he is or was or how many kids you have. He is a scourge. He is despicable. Most importantly, he is a coward for not being man enough to end the relationship. If you let him have his cake and eat it too, he will. And, you just reinforced his horrible behavior. Cut him loose, girls. He doesn't deserve you. If he says he cheated because you were a lousy lay, ignore him. He says that to every girl he does this to. Cheater guys are another cancer on society. They breed mistrust and suspicion. They are thicker than thieves. They might fool you your entire time together but that makes them even more repulsive. On the other hand, if you go for a guy who is a DJ at a strip club and he screws one of the strippers, then that's your oversight. Stay away from sleazy, low rent, unkempt cheaters and their squeaky clean white-collar counterparts. They don't deserve you. If you can't figure out for sure if he's a cheater, hire a private investigator. Its not as expensive as you think. If you are married it is absolutely worth it. If you have kids, you better find out where he really is. What if there was an emergency with one of the kids? Even worse, what if he was in mid-coitus while you were frantically trying to call him? If you find anything, anywhere that belongs to a woman or if you smell perfume on anything and he babbles some lame excuse or explanation, red flag. Oh, and any guy who waits until you are asleep or gone to get online or goes to another room to use the computer is up to no good. Heavy facebooking and myspacing if you are a guy in a relationship is uncommon. Look into it. If he let's you look at his profiles, notice how he presents himself. Does it say anything about you? Does it say "relationship" in the relationship status area? Are there girls all over everywhere responding to him? If so, he is flirting and probably scheming on how to get one or more of the girls to sleep with him. If he acts guarded and secretive about myspace and facebook, duh! He's obviously up to something, ladies. Come on. Why would he get that mad? Why would he wait to get online? Why would he hide his cell phone screen or leave it locked when its on the charger or he is asleep? Use your head. If he turns his phone off every time you hang out its so the other girl can't call. If you think he is full of shit when you ask him what he and his guy friends did when you went out of town for Thanksgiving you are probably onto something. Cheaters suck. If you have had it happen once that's all it takes. Nothing feels worse. You feel so violated and disgusted. Then, you are floored by the molten rejection and dismissal of your body. Then, the questioning starts: was it my fault? Did I not listen to his needs? Did my weight gain from the holidays turn him off? Oh my god, I bet he has been doing this the whole time! I wondered why he was so eager for me to go on that camping thing with my girlfriends last Fall? That bastard. And, so on and so forth. I also don't recommend telling guys you have just started dating all about your cheating ex or ex-husband or lousy ex. It's sort of an unfortunate turn off. No guy wants to get involved with a girl they think goes for cheaters or losers. I know it wasn't your fault but trust me on this: guys don't need to know the real reason you broke up. Mention that he broke one of your rules and if you get pushed to say which one say he betrayed your trust. Let your new guy fill in the blanks. Good guys will cringe after pushing you to answer. But, they will rejoice that they have a shot with you because some other dude screwed it up. So, keep your new guy in mind if you tend to go on and on about your sorry ex-boyfriend who cheated on you hardcore. Nobody wants to listen to that shit for too long. We get it that it sucked and that he is horrible for doing that to you. But, let's move forward or stop and let you heal. Either way cheaters don't deserve the power you give them to disrupt or destroy your right to future love. Cheaters will pay the price one day. Karma never forgets or leaves anyone out. Let karma get him and move on. He will cross the wrong woman one day and she will blow his brains out. Don't let your life get ruined over a cheating scumbag. Just drop them, tell everyone you know that knew him that he is a cheater and that's why you ended it and move on.

5. The Mystery Man- this is the Roger Moore of the dating world. He can turn out to be an Austin Powers-like dork once you get to his core. But, he keeps you in suspense. He is hard to read or unreadable. He kisses you and holds you but he hasn't made a big move. He has cool friends, a real job, he is single and emotionally available. He keeps you atwitter with girlie giggles at his sexy

text messages and sultry voicemails. The Mystery Man is the archetype of the guy you want so bad but you have no earthly idea how they feel about you. They make you bide time as they seduce, lure, and taunt you. They keep you on your toes when you go out. They make you stutter and stammer, your knees grow weak with his every breathy word. He is romance. He is the enigma of love. He is your White Whale. You may be smitten through and through but ladies? If you don't confront him after a few months of dating about where he's at and how he feels about you and get a firm answer, move on. The mystery is no mystery to me. Guys that string you along and epitomize the term "cock tease" are really just scared to get close. They learned after getting burned by some seductress long before you that keeping women in suspense about how they feel is a great way to wield power in the relationship. The Mystery Man makes you wonder how and why he is single? The answer is he is afraid to commit because he got burned bad somewhere along the way. Maybe his Mommy didn't hold him enough or his ex broke his heart after he opened up to her finally? Either way, if any guy you are with keeps you in suspense about how they feel about you that is in effect the same thing as any other barrier or obstacle to one's heart. It comes from a wounded place that has festered. Don't let them string you along forever. Make him decide. Tell him you won't hurt him and its okay to share his heart. If he can't or won't, turn him loose, back to the shadows to seduce his next hapless victim. But, once he's gone, try seeing him for what he really was: afraid. Mystique and seduction are key ingredients when getting to know someone new. But, if the mystery prevails after six to eight months and you have no freaking idea how he feels about you, I say confront him. Tell him you love his spy-like appeal but that you kinda need to know where he stands. He will either evaporate into mist or he will roll over and reveal his soft underbelly. If he presents belly, rub it gently. There might be a good guy underneath that mystique but usually they are just dorks.

Chapter Summary: Okay girls, let's review. First, we talked about how guys act in the beginning of the relationship using their style and patterns of contact and behavior around you as a litmus for their worthiness as a potential mate or boyfriend. Then, I taught you how to spot Players and when you have been duped by one. We moved into how to handle your current bad relationship, if you are stuck in one. Then, we moved on to discuss the lowly Cheater and how to salt his game, for good. I gave you one of the most important dating tips of the whole book, don't talk about your lousy ex when just starting out with a new guy. Don't do it, it is a major turn off. Going on about your ex makes the new guy question your emotional availability. We concluded with a discussion of how to handle the guy who keeps you guessing. Now its time for your homework. I want you to think back on all your past relationships and see what kind of guys you have been drawn to. For example, does it seem like every relationship you end is over a cheating lover? Are you getting played by Players over and over? Are you in a relationship right now that sucks when it used to be awesome? Have you always done that in relationships? Are you or have you ever been suspicious that your guy is a cheater? Do you do that with every relationship? What type of men are you going for? Rich, poor, artsy, refined, democrat, republican, atheist, Christian, family man or bachelor? What adjectives describe the guy you want after reading so far and examining the evidence? Do you have some new Red Flags to add to your list? Do it now. Write down anything that helps you get clarity on this major part of your life. Review what you have written. Find a buddy to talk it through with, somebody that knows you well. At the end of the day, crack open a bottle of wine and unwind. Give yourself a day off to not think about silly guys and all their problems. Because the next chapter we are going in. That's right. I'm going to turn the microscope on you.

Chapter You!--

You. Beautiful you. The most important
person you know the best. Let's help her
get better at loving herself.
Exercise 1- Go look in the mirror. Stand
there for a solid three or four minutes. I
want you to look into your own eyes.
Stare deep. Remember the little girl you
once were and the woman you are now.
Think about your precious life. All of it.
The joy, the sorrow, the highs, the lows,
the things you love doing, the people
who are or were good to you, and where
you are now, with all of it. Are you
happy? Are you depressed? Are you
content with your life? What should you
keep? What should you change? What
have you struggled with? What makes
you feel passion? If you are in tears now
get yourself a tissue then a behavioral
therapist. Go ahead. The book will be
here waiting. Is getting into a
relationship a good idea right now for
you? Be honest. I can't be there to stop
you from lying to yourself. After you
have taken a close look, I want you to
decide now what to do.
Exercise 2-- Write down your plan for
change and follow it. If it means ending

a relationship to get you happy, do it. If it means you have to relocate, change careers, change your life, lose some friends, or otherwise come out of that cocoon you have been in then butterfly please. The world needs to see that beauty you had wrapped in silky despair for all those years. Unfurl your new wings and take flight. If you encounter fear, fly above it. If that guy you finally got rid of begs you back and curses my name, soar above his cries. Take yourself to the new island. I showed you what it looked like. We took the deluxe tour. I showed you the truth about men. Don't become a moth who blindly flies into the burning light of love, stay the butterfly fluttering close enough to get warm but never close enough to get burned. You have been writing in that notepad. Right? If you haven't then I failed. All changes start with a contract. That notepad is your new contract. Get into it. Don't neglect that part of the book. It is critical that you write things down in order to see it actualized on paper. Sometimes when you write something down and read it back to yourself you finally see how deluded you've been. Don't stay in that fantasy world of pain that comes from lying to yourself. As a therapist, I can tell you after ten years, the worst lies people tell are the ones they tell themselves.

So, stop doing that if you are guilty of that crime. Get honest. Get a plan. Get results. If you are going to date online be thorough with screening your dates. Never give them your phone number or address on the first date. Block your phone number or call them from a pay phone. Tell them you want a background check to make sure they are safe. If they won't do it or if they laugh at you, hang up and move on. I cannot bear the thought of one of my beloved readers getting hurt by some psycho who has a credit card and Internet access to the same dating site as you. If you have any Red Flags pop up during your pre-date emails or conversation(s) skip this guy. The good thing about online dating is there are plenty of guys to choose from. If you feel good about a first date be sure to meet up in a busy, public place during the day, with plenty of people around. Have your guy hand you the background check. If there's anything you don't like about it, fake a phone call and say its an emergency and you've gotta go. Never look back. Be overly suspicious and leery of guys who date online. It is fertile ground for relationship addicts, heavy substance addicts, and creeps. Don't hang out alone with anybody you meet online without letting somebody know where you are, at all times. If the guy bitches about that, say goodnight. Your safety and well being are never worth pleasing a stranger who begs and pleads with you to come home with them after only a few dates. Try to meet their friends, colleagues, or family. If they seem normal and sane that's usually a good sign. If they have no friends, stay away. That's crazy. If you meet up with online guys who you have never met in person and don't arm yourself with something, don't blame me if something goes wrong, eventually. Get MACE for your purse. The Internet is a perfect place for crazy killers and stalkers. They have unlimited access to the same websites as you. What makes you think they wouldn't go online to date or meet victims? Don't chance it. Be paranoid. Ask a lot of questions. Watch out for Red Flags. Never ever meet up with a stranger at a hotel or on the beach or in a park at night or anything

like that. You never know who you're
getting. Be careful. Date rape is still
extremely common. Guys can use fake
names online and in person. Guys can
drop drugs in your drink. You never
know. If you do go to his house never
drink anything that you didn't open
yourself. Opt for a beer instead of a
cocktail or glass of wine. If he pushes
you to drink something from a glass,
leave. Always sit closer to the door than
he does. That way if he does something
crazy you have a chance to make it out.
If he is getting too fresh too fast and you
are getting scared or uncomfortable, get
out of there. Lie. Say you forgot about
an early work meeting and scram.
Pushy guys who just want sex can get
violent or nasty once rejected. Don't let
him push you into sex if you aren't
ready, get out of there. The Player loves
online dating, too. He might be
awesome, fun, nice, sane, sexy, stable,
and desirable. He might possess every
quality you want. But, sniff around
carefully. You might be tonight's entree.
And, he might have tomorrow's entree
lined up and waiting in the wings. Ask
how often he dates. If he says
something vague or nonsensical, he's a

player. If he says he loves being a bachelor and can see himself living this way for good but that he has needs and you have needs and you guys should be able to handle having sex for fun just know he has used that same spiel on every girl he's played so far and they all fell for it, got sucked in, asked him to commit and he said no because he told you in the beginning he was a bachelor. The Player creates the illusion of hope. He is a mirage in the desert. Once you run to him and he turns invisible you will see. You just got played and it hurts. So, be careful.

Exercise 3-- Enact your plan for change. Your goals should include some things around self-care and repair. If you are still wounded from your last relationship, stay away from guys until you are ready. If you are too scared to date online try singles mixers, speed dating, table for six, clubs, bars, and concerts. Guys will talk to you. If they don't, you talk to them. Keep it simple. Make a comment about the place where you're both hanging out. See if he bites. If not, don't despair. Do what guys do: just move to the next one. Eventually, you will find a modern Prince Charming. Never give up. There are billions of men. Some good, some great, but most are deplorable wraiths. Use your Red Flags to eliminate the bad ones and work on yourself. Listen to your gut first and then your heart. Follow the one who pleads the best case. Don't get blinded by the light of love, squint a little and see what lies beneath. Guys who cheat or are jerks will always be there to hit on you at every turn in the road but I say wade through that sea to reach your new shore. And, take notes along the way. Never miss an opportunity for growth and health through writing. Know that pain is a part of love. Most of all, don't miss out on getting to know yourself in relation to relationships. Forge your own identity, separate from him. You will thank me later. Women whose only life is their husband are at a huge disadvantage when that fairytale ends with him screwing a twenty year-old and getting caught. Divorce might cripple you. Break ups might leave you hopeless and depressed but try to keep your eyes on the prize. Know that somewhere right now there is some awesome guy who will make you his Princess and ultimately his Queen. It is

your job to find him in the labyrinth of
love.

Fail-Proof Dating Tips:

1. Don't be nervous, be at their service. Everybody gets nervous before or during dates. Don't focus on the anxiety, focus on the conversation. Your being at his service means you are attentive to the conversation, not your own jitters. You are blocking out the nervous to service the conversation. Get it? Got it? Good. Stop fretting. Too much anxiety means you're not ready to date. Work on being secure within yourself before claiming to be ready for love with another. Girls who are too shy or too chatty are annoying. Float in the middle. Say too much and risk overwhelming the poor guy, don't say anything and risk losing him altogether. Nerves mean uncertainty or fear. They affect the vibe. Get a handle on them or risk scaring off Mr. Right.

2. How to dispel feeling unattractive: a step-by-step mini-guide. Rule #1: Everybody has something sexy about them. Find yours. Show it off. If you think you are flat-chested but you have a nice booty, wear tighter pants or a skirt to show off that nice

booty. If you are heavy set but have a generous bust, show them off. If you feel frumpy and don't have boobs or booty, wear make-up to show off your smile and eyes. If you don't think you look sexy, act sexy. Ladies? I know some of you hate your bodies or think guys won't have sex with you. You're wrong. If you don't believe me, try the following exercise: Go online to Craig's List. Place an ad for a Casual Encounter. In it, talk as filthy as you'd like about all the sexy things you are good at in bed. Your computer will melt with responses from men. If you think you are "ugly" or have no physical features that are sexy, act sexy. Do the best with what you were given and let your words and acts seduce for you. One of the only perks to online dating is the email correspondence can get pretty steamy before or after the dates. Use your words to be sexy. The written word is the original aphrodisiac. Flattery will get you everywhere. If you are worried about your looks, let your acts take over. Sexy acts can be just as sexy as sexy looks. If you can't tap into that part of your sexual self while retaining dignity and worth, take a break from dating to get that squared away in therapy. If a guy makes or has ever made you feel ugly or says things that make you feel unattractive for any reason at any point in a relationship, get out. If you have sex with a guy and his reaction to your naked body the first time makes you feel ugly, do something. If you're heavy, lose weight. If you're skinny, pick your sexiest feature and show it off more. Try shaving down there. If you have no butt and no boobs, do something. Drop or gain weight. Something will pop out or in! If you just look the way you do and that's how God made you, know there are guys who feel the same way about themselves. Find him online using a dating service. Hold your picture up next to his. Do you guys look like a good match? Once you get close to him (after you've both been tested for STDs, all daters should get tested before sexual activity), you will have great sex, once you tap into your sexual selves.

You will find out how beautiful you really are and how wrong you were to think love would forget you. Our youth-obsessed culture makes us all ugly by comparison. Embrace diversity. The media, Internet, advertising, television, global society, and most sexist men say young is beautiful, eternal, and the exemplar of life. If life is best lived by the most beautiful, why do we have a pandemic of Body Dysmorphic Disorder fueled plastic surgery? So, let's leave looks out of your self-worth estimations. Find what you think is sexy about you and peacock those feathers. If you have to get in shape to get a guy, do it. If you tried the gym and quit, go back. If you are lazy and expect short cuts and quick-fix diets to work, they won't. Exercise hard four days a week for at least twenty minutes. Get hardcore. If you have to dress a little sexier, do it. If you have to turn off the lights to talk dirty, do it. Find your sexy. Express and embrace it. God gave everybody something sexy, sometimes you have to flip a switch and open your mind or mouth to find it. Rule #2: If

you can't get guys to talk to you, try
talking to them. This rule is for all the
"hotties" who complain about guys
never talking to them. Ladies? We
know her. She is gorgeous. She
causes the music to stop when she
walks in the bar. But, believe it or
not, she's single! She is too hot to
trot! Guys won't talk to her. She
clings to her group of girls. They
close down the bar. She goes home
drunk and alone. She puts on her
pajamas, pours a nightcap, turns on
TV, and eventually goes to sleep by
herself. Everybody loves her.
Nobody can figure out why she's
single? Years go by. Let me stop
you. You foxy ladies are afraid of
rejection, too. Its okay. Welcome to
our world. The solution is simple. If
guys aren't talking to you, try talking
to them. Gorgeous, lonely women
feel entitled to men's advances. The
problem is guys are convinced you
are taken because you are scorching
hot and so into talking with and
hanging right near your girlfriends.
Or, when you're out somewhere
alone, you put off the "I'm too hot for
you" vibe. Be mindful of how you

carry yourself. Try talking about something light. You don't have to launch into religion and politics, just be natural. Guys will respond. Some will babble and stammer because a good looking girl talked to them first but that will pass. Get over yourself if you are lonely and gorgeous. If you make men climb your tower but you refuse to come down from it once they make the ascent then don't complain about ending up at the top alone and grey someday. Looks fade. Personality does not. If you are gorgeous but unapproachable, it won't stay that way. Unapproachable will win out. If you don't open up to those around you and come down from the heights, you'll grow old up there. The reason hideous guys land gorgeous women is because they talked to them when other better looking guys shied away. They had nothing to lose, due to being hideous, so they went for it while the better guy for her feared the vibe she put off. This rule also applies to women who are impossible to please or set up. If you are picky and remain single because you are "too pretty for him" it won't last. Every year that goes by is another year lost to your own vanity. Get over yourself. You won't stay golden forever. You will turn brown in the sun. Beauty fades. Find out what getting to know a person beneath their body is like and you will have success. Rule #3: Attractive is a state of mind and finance. When do we feel our sexiest? When we have money and the perfect outfit on, right? Looking good is feeling good. Ladies? If you are struggling financially and dating is tough, do your best with what you have. If you can swing It, use dating as a way to experiment with new looks! Maybe your ex-boyfriend made you self-conscious about your cleavage? But, you've got a hot date who's a little out of your league this Friday night and you want to take it to the next level. Go get that low cut blouse you saw at the Mall! Right now! Put the book down! Why? Because you deserve it. You deserve to look sexy for a guy you like who might one day father your children or be there for you for the rest of your life. Dating is an investment in your future. Dating is shopping for the future. Improve your odds of finding the best match by looking your best and achieving your peak confidence. You will frighten the non-committal away. You will draw the true hearted nearer. You will show up to the date happy, confident, and feeling rich. That's sexy in action. Get it girls. Rule #4: When all else fails, throw sex at it. If you feel "ugly" but the guy you're seeing isn't shy, try going along with it! If you are chronically single due to feeling unattractive/ ugly/unworthy what do you have to lose? Let the guy who thinks you're sexy show you on your body with his how he feels. Maybe over time you will break down and realize attractive or not isn't as important as how connected two people in love can be? If your feeling sexy or attractive isn't a problem for him, try going with it. Love will eventually blind you to those false feelings you have about your body. Give it or him a chance to change your view or stay lonely. Your choice. Rule #5: Dress sexier. If you aren't getting a response from guys try dressing sexier. Just do it. It works. Get those boots out. Lose the frumpy jeans. Squeeze into that skirt. Do your make-up extra sexy. Guys love it. Other women hate it. But, it works on your potential mate. Remember: you are going after him, not her. Stop worrying about what the girls think when you are gussied up for a cute boy you want to be sexual with. If he is into it, mission accomplished. Those women clowning you for your outfit are home alone or with their jerk husbands who dog them the same way. Forget them. Look at Nature. If a mate wants a potential mate, they have to stand out. Doll up. Go shop at the risqué store you avoided when you were with your boring ex. Do whatever it takes to embody sexy and you will exude confidence. I don't care what body type you have or want. Guys will sleep with you. If you want unfulfilling sex, go online and find them. If you want long-term love making with a mate, embrace and invest in your look. You are trying to attract a mate. Look like it.

3. More Fashion tips: Rule #1: No Hats. Sorry, ladies, but the vast majority of

hats detract from your desired look. Stay away from hats. They are too risky to wear out on dates. They might ruin your chances with a good guy due to looking stupid to him, not you. Headbands, visors, glasses, and all hair holding accessories that serve a functional purpose, like keeping hair out of your face, are fine but pick sexy ones. Why go for a dull bl headband that serves a function but has no fashion? Go for both function and fashion. Glasses can be smoking hot. Think sheik not librarian when picking out new frames. Some hats are safer than others to wear out if you must. Baseball caps worn forward with a ponytail out the back hole can be sexy on girls. A fitted baseball cap worn backwards can be sexy on the right girl. But, why roll the dice? Wait til you've got a steady boyfriend then go hat crazy. Dating should be hat-free. Its a fashion gamble you need not take. If you can't agree, do me a solid: try dates with and without your hats to see how they differ. Sadly, the hat sends the message of needing to cover something up. For men, it is almost always their balding they cover with hats. For women, men don't know what it is, therefore, the hat can become a deal breaker if it hides its secret for too long. Try it out if you don't believe me. Layering ten scarves, getting really long, fake overdone nails, painting on gaudy make-up, too many facial piercings, and wearing too much jewelry are all looks to be avoided regardless of season as well. Rule #2: Don't wear rings on your ring fingers! This one should be obvious. But, its not. You see it all the time. If you are single, take off those damn ring finger rings! You are confusing us! We don't know if its okay to approach! The first thing a gentlemen does is check a lady's hand for rings with a glance. If she is married or engaged, he respects that. If he does not see a ring, it means "single and approachable." If you are wearing anything on that finger, no matter how obvious it may be to you that its not a wedding or engagement ring, he will defer approaching you to avoid being wrong. Guys will see rings on either hand on a ring finger and check you

off the list of girls to talk to. As a
matter of fact, you can try wearing
rings and not wearing them when
you're out to see how men treat you.
Watch their eyes. They will almost
always sneak a peak at your hands.
It is not a conscious process. If you
need a break from dating, wear a
ring on your left ring finger when
you're out with friends for a night.
You will probably be left alone. Don't
forget before the date: check your
fingers and fingernails. If you have
gnarly gunk under your nails, get it
now. Don't wait, you'll forget. Rule
#3: Let colors show off your features,
not detract from them. Loud colors
look cool. Sometimes they look
great. In the right season, at the right
place, they can make an outfit. But,
like the hat, they are a fashion
gamble. That tight, neon pink
sweater looks great on the rack. You
think it looks great on you. You go
out. Date ends. Guy doesn't call. He
laughs instead to his friends about
"pink sweater girl from online" who
looked ridiculous at his local bar as
no one was wearing anything like
that. There was a ballgame on and

local team colors prevailed. The lesson is: you never know where a date will end up. In the beginning, or pre-sex phase of dating someone, stay away from loud colors. Fashion gamble, not worth it. Try earth tones. Go for rich, dark greens, browns, blues, and crisp black. There's nothing sexier than black. Black hides the heavy set dater. Black is slimming when featured up top or in tight pants. White does the opposite. White and tight is okay. All the colors of the rainbow are fair game but in the beginning, stay color quiet, unless you are trying to be sexier for self-esteem reasons. Gray is a fashion gamble. Darker gray is less of a gamble but light gray should follow the rule of whites which is white and tight is fine. Let garments accentuate your figure. Do not hide behind garments. Avoid garments that drape or hang over your frame. Go for tighter fitting clothes. Men want to see your body. Fact: if you keep hiding your body behind clothes that drape, men will move on to the next dater. Lose the shame. Show off something. Stop hiding it.

Stay away from garments with bows, tacky sequins, shoulder pads, visible elastic bands, gaudy seasonal embroidery, saches, trinkets, and excessive, bunched, or shiny material of any kind. Stay away from stone washed denim. It is still tacky. Stay away from t-shirts that are too big, looks frumpy. Avoid big, clunky shoes. Guys are not looking at or impressed by shoes, girls. I'm sorry. We don't care. Wear shoes on dates that can go anywhere. When you are dating someone new, dress for anything. Spontaneous fun from dates in the beginning of the relationship makes lifelong memories of how you fell in love what they are. If you ruin spontaneity because of your stupid clunky shoes that kept you from taking that romantic beach walk then you might have let fashion cost you a mate! Rule #4: Don't wear sandals on dates either. You will anyway. But, I suggest you have footwear that gives you full access to any activity. Why? Guys will have something planned for your date and glance down to see you have sandals with no socks and they'll have to rethink. Example: a new guy you are gaga over after four dates wants to take you bowling after dinner at the Sushi bar. You show up to the restaurant wearing sandals with no socks. So much for bowling! Plan "B" means you go to a lousy movie and drop buttered popcorn on your toes the whole time. The guy is miffed. His fun plans got dashed and instead he had to give you the shitty dinner-and-a-movie date. He decides to log back onto eHarmony for another dater. He doesn't even bother to call you. He sends you the generic "thanks for the date, I'll be in touch" email and he's off. Unless you know you are going to a fancy dinner followed by a night on the town, stay away from shoes that restrict your gait and activity options when dating. Usually daters will plan their outings but in the beginning wear clothes for anything. Rule #5: If you know what activites have been planned for the date, dress accordingly! It could be as simple as remembering to wear jeans and carry your wallet, not your purse because you guys are trying rock climbing at the mall. It could also be choosing the right outfit for the activity. Ladies? If he is dropping some big bucks to take you somewhere decent or nice, dress up. Stay conservative, no loud colors, but make your clothes match the activity. Don't go for a day at Six Flags wearing high heels, pearls, and a prom dress. Dress for what the date requires. If you are a diva and are trying to date an outdoorsmen, it ain't gonna work. Change clothes or change guys. Oh, and any guy who makes you pay for any part of any date is cheap. Drop him. Men have to invest in their future, too. Let him. Broke dudes or guys without regular pay are off limits. They can't committ to an finding an income, what makes you think you will become top priority? You won't. Don't go for guys who have no means. If he sucks you in, you will foot the bill for that relationship. Mooching is mooching, those guys are bad. Guys who let you pay are worse. Cheap guys hoard affection, too. Stay away. Get a guy with a real job.

4. Etiquette tips, how to act on the date: Rule #1: Shut up about your Ex. We

don't care. We don't want to hear about him or them. Ladies? We know he is a scumbag. We know he broke your heart or got on your nerves. We know you are so happy to finally be away from him. Then, why do you keep talking about him? Exactly. Stop. It ruins dates. If you compulsively talk about your Ex(s), you should stop dating until you recover from the loss(es) of that/those relationship(s). Follow that formula. Rule #2: Stop dogging men. Stop making fun of men, talking about how sorry they are, talking about how they're all full of shit. Stop or the translation to your date becomes: "If all men are so terrible, why are we on this date?" Rule #3: We are not interested in hearing about other people you know and their problems, for too long. Don't subject your date to your girlfriend's relationship stuff or any other lengthy description about other people especially on the first date. They will think: "I thought we were supposed to get to know each other? Why am I hearing about some friend of yours I don't know and their problems? Talk about you. Talk or ask about me. Some short stories about friends are fine but don't go on for forever. It is boring to listen to. Talk about your hobbies, goals, and dreams or inquire about mine. Don't give me a forty minute speech about your friend who just got dumped. I feign interest and sympathy, the truth is, I don't know that person. I'm not on a date with them, I'm on a date with you." Other topics to avoid on the first few dates include: heated political issues, deep or divisive religious debates, the death penalty, your sexual past, their sexual past, any history of mental collapse or breakdown you may have had, being in therapy, and any domestic violence or crazy boyfriend stories. Discussing medical problems or anything gross around and during meals is also off limits. No one wants to hear gnarly detailed medical crap while they are trying to eat! Another huge no-no is cell phone calls and texts. Stay off the phone on dates, it is utterly rude. If you can't put your phone down long enough to form a relationship, pass this book to a friend. I can't do anything for you. Rule #4: Do not bombard us with negativity. Negative women are just as bad as the "Robert Downer JR.'s" out there. Negative women talk about their crappy job, their lousy friends, their lack of a social life, and how life sucks when you are them. No thanks. Sometimes they dress it up with humor but the underlying messages are loud and clear. Negative women emit the "I'm so miserable bet you can't fix me" charm most men sniff out early. They might stick around long enough to get to the sex but soon after, the negativity turns them off. If you joke about yourself in a self-deprecating way and have nothing nice to say about anyone or anything, you are depressed. Guys are picking up on it. That's why you're alone. We listen to you dog yourself, your life, your job, your friends, your family and the future. It gets old, dude. Stop it. Talk about something that gives you pleasure. Try being hopeful, positive, and have fun for God's sake. Is life that bad? If it is, get used to bitching about it to no one. You won't find any ear but that of another miser. If you have a scowl on your face, are rolling your eyes or shaking your head reading this, I'm talking to you. Rule #5: If you are not into a guy after being a little sexual, be delicate with their feelings if you decide to end it. There's no reason to hurt feelings when dating. If you decide to share a good night kiss and your date wants more but you don't, go easy. Be clear. Be honest. But, don't put guys down or shame them excessively when rejecting them. Why? Because it shows poor form. A mature, refined woman doesn't need to shame or name call. She excuses herself and the night ends. The suitor gets the message without unnecessary harm.

5. Final thoughts about dating: Rule #1- You are more important than anyone else. If you are happy being single but your family won't stop pressuring you to date and marry, put your foot down. If they bought you this book hoping you would take a hint but you don't need a man show them this sentence: Dr. Ray says to mind your own beeswax.

You are in charge of you. If you choose to be single and you got this book from a pushy Mom or Grandma, I'm sorry. I didn't write it for them to poke you with. I want you to stay solo if that's what makes you happy for now. If or when you get ready, the book will be here. Rule #2: Never stay with a guy who hits. If he hits you for any reason over anything, end it. Never give him a second chance. Don't be a sucker for him to punch. Guys who hit women are worse than cheaters but not by much. Rule #3: If he cheats and you stay, he repeats. If you allow him back after busting him or having him tell you he cheated, he will burn you again or hide his cheating better. Cheaters are like beaters, they don't deserve forgiveness or a second chance. They taint love with their actions. If you let them get away with that you are just as wrong as they are. Stop letting him back in your house, your heart, and your bed. Cheaters, beaters, drunks, deserters, and players are all cowards at their core. Don't let him have the joy and relief from forgiveness. Drop him or suffer the consequences. Rule #4: Don't feel bad for too long if you had to end a long term

83

marriage or relationship to be single. Sometimes you leave a jagged edge. Sometimes he falls apart, bad. Sometimes your kids turn on you. But, if you were unhappy for that long for any reason, it was the right choice to end it. Your former lover may be inconsolable. That is not your fault forever. It is up to them to move on, at some point. You have the right to be happy, even if that right makes others unhappy, temporarily. Rule #5: If you are ever assaulted on a date, attack the eyes, throat, genitals, and fight for your life. Women in urban areas should take a rape prevention self-defense course. All daters need to buy a keychain-sized MACE.

Pat Benitar said it best, "Love is a battlefield." Be ready to fight using your head and heart. Be on guard when getting to know online daters. Be positive. Dress to show off your sexy or act out your sexy. Be yourself. Be natural. Be confident. Get informed about the dater you're with. Invest in your future carefully. The time spent with someone wrong while the right person is waiting for you is time you can't get back. Don't settle. Don't jump the gun. Go with your gut. Butterfly and peacock your way into his heart. Plant the seed of love. Water. Watch grow... Care for daily... Enjoy...

Dedication: To every child of divorce...I
wish I could wipe away your tears...

www.ingramcontent.com/pod-product-compliance
Lightning Source LLC
Chambersburg PA
CBHW051209050326
40689CB00008B/1252